THOMAS JEFFERSON

The Declaration of Independence
and the Expansion of US Territory

Written by Aude Perrineau
In collaboration with Guillaume Hairy
Translated by Rose Brichard

History 50MINUTES.com

THOMAS JEFFERSON

KEY INFORMATION

- **Born:** 13 April 1743 in Albermarle County (Virginia).
- **Died:** 4 July 1826 in Monticello (Virginia).
- **Political party:** The Democratic-Republican Party.
- **Dates of election:**
    - 17 February 1801
    - 5 December 1804.
- **Length of presidency:** 8 years.
- **Main achievements:**
    - Drafting of the Declaration of Independence
    - Limiting the federal government's powers
    - The Louisiana Purchase
    - The Lewis and Clark Expedition.

INTRODUCTION

Thomas Jefferson was one of America's Founding Fathers. Like George Washington (1732-1799), under whom he served as Secretary of State between 1789 and 1795, Jefferson was a landowner hailing from Virginia. Jefferson not only contributed to the development of the Virginia state constitution, he was a talented political writer and the principal author of the Declaration of Independence.

He served as vice president under John Adams (1735-1826) before being elected as president in 1801. While his predecessors had established a federalist basis for the American system, Jefferson entrenched the institutions of power in a resolutely republican ideology.

He is also responsible for the United States' purchase of Louisiana, which doubled the size of American national territory. Furthermore, his initiatives were the first chapter of the epic tale which would come to construct the American identity, namely the conquest of the West, led by Meriwether Lewis (American soldier and explorer, 1774-1809) and William Clark (American explorer, 1770-1838). A cultivated intellectual with a thirst for knowledge, Jefferson dedicated the latter stages of his life to founding the University of Virginia.

DID YOU KNOW?

The term "Founding Fathers" refers to the 56 signatories of the Declaration of Independence, including John Adams, Benjamin Franklin (American philosopher, physician and statesman, 1706-1790) and Thomas Jefferson.

BIOGRAPHY

Portrait of Thomas Jefferson by Mather Brown.

A PRIVILEGED UPBRINGING

Thomas Jefferson was born on 13 April 1743 in Albemarle County. His father Peter Jefferson (1708-1757) was a planter, surveyor, commander of the local militia and political actor. His mother Jane Randolph (1721-1776) hailed from a rich Virginian family. The young Thomas therefore grew up in a wealthy and respected family in a well-healed social sphere. In 1757 when he was just 14, his father died, leaving the young Thomas to inherit the plantation.

In 1760, he began attending William and Mary College, where he received a rigorous classical education, ranging from philosophy to the ancient languages - for which he had a particular passion - and from literature to science. This education was strongly influenced by Enlightenment thinking, which posits reason as the central and utmost source of authority. Jefferson then set his sights on a legal career, taking the Virginia bar in 1767. His scholarly output was more greatly appreciated by his contemporaries than his talents as an orator, and Jefferson quickly established himself in the professional and intellectual sphere. His approach to law, characterised by a more socio-political perspective, was particularly noted by those around him.

ENTRANCE ONTO THE POLITICAL SCENE

In 1792 Jefferson married Martha Wayles Skelton (1748-1782), the widowed daughter of a prominent attorney. The two set up their little home in the heart of Jefferson's plantations, which he had named Monticello. He had an avid interest in

architecture and took it upon himself to extend and recons-
truct the building over several years. It eventually stood as a
vast structure inspired by Venetian and French architecture.

Photograph of Monticello as it currently stands.

As a member of the Virginia House of Burgesses (which was
to become the state General Assembly), Jefferson distinguished himself through his strong standpoint against British
colonial rule. It was with this political outlook that he
drafted *A Summary View of the Rights of British America* to
guide Virginian delegates at the First Continental Congress.
Though Jefferson's outlined positions were seen as too
radical to be adopted, the pamphlet was distributed in
London, New York and Philadelphia; the young Jefferson had
earned himself a reputation. This led to him being selected
by the Second Continental Congress in 1776 to draft the
Declaration of Independence with Benjamin Franklin, John
Adams, Roger Sherman (American lawyer and statesman,
1721-1793) and Robert Livingston (American statesman,

1746-1813).

Writing the Declaration of Independence, 1776, painting by Jean Leon Gerome Ferris, depicting (from left to right) Benjamin Franklin, John Adams and Thomas Jefferson.

During Jefferson's term as governor of Virginia which coincided with the American Revolution (1775-1782), the British invaded the state. Unlike his contemporary George Washington who distinguished himself on the battlefield, Thomas Jefferson was strongly criticised for his cowardice in fleeing Charlottesville to evade capture. He returned to Monticello where he authored *Notes on the State of Virginia*, a text in which he outlines the state territory and its political ideals, focussing notably on religion, education and slavery.

Jefferson represented the state of Virginia at the Congress of the Confederation (successor of the Second Continental Congress) in 1783, where he unsuccessfully defended the decimalisation of currency and the rejection of the Northwest Ordinance, ratified in 1787. This act formalised the potential for negotiation with Native American tribes for territorial purposes and established the requirements of statehood.

In 1785 Jefferson was appointed Minister to France, succeeding Benjamin Franklin. He greatly admired French culture, and this position allowed him first-hand experience of the first whispers of the French revolution to come (1789). It also inspired a powerful correspondence between he and his friend James Madison (who would become President of the United States, 1751-1836). Jefferson approved the American Constitution, signed in 1787, but was careful to underline that it would need certain changes in order to fully protect basic freedoms.

When George Washington was elected the first President of the United States of America, Jefferson was appointed as Secretary of State. Despite Washington's total confidence in him, Jefferson's political standpoints were regularly undermined, such as his support for France, his mistrust of Britain and the country's economic direction, the latter informed by the transfer of support from Secretary of State to Treasury Secretary Alexander Hamilton (1755-1804). Jefferson objected to Hamilton's "federalist" ideology, and laid the foundation for what would become the Democratic-Republican Party.

THE PRESIDENTIAL ELECTIONS

In the elections following the end of Washington's presidential term, Jefferson was runner-up to John Adams, under whom he served as vice president until 1801. The two men had a tumultuous relationship, Jefferson regularly disagreeing with the president's decisions particularly with regards to the Alien and Sedition Acts (1798). It was around this time that Jefferson penned the Kentucky resolutions, which brought to light the possibility for a state to deem a federal law unconstitutional. Though the bill was not adopted, it would serve as a basis for congressional activities for years to come.

Following the end of John Adams' mandate, Jefferson was elected president in February 1801 and again in November 1804. During his eight-year term, he reduced defence spending on the army and navy, put an end to the taxes which had provoked riots under the presidencies of his predecessors and even managed to reduce the national debt. In 1803 he purchased Louisiana from Napoleon Bonaparte (French emperor, 1769-1821) and organised an expedition to new territories with the help of his personal adviser Meriwether Lewis. These actions led to the territory of the United States doubling in size.

With regards to foreign policy, Jefferson remained resolutely neutral towards the emerging conflict between France and Great Britain (1793-1802).

At the end of his second term in March 1809, Jefferson, like Washington before him, decided not to run for another consecutive term and retired to Monticello, where he dedicated himself fully to his passions for knowledge and culture by establishing the University of Virginia, inaugurated in 1819. Jefferson died on 4 July 1826 on the fiftieth anniversary of the Declaration of Independence.

POLITICAL, SOCIAL AND ECONOMIC CONTEXT

DEBATES ON A FEDERALIST POLITICAL ECONOMY

At the beginning of the 19th century, agriculture dominated the US economy. Nine out of ten Americans worked in this area, most of them in the South or in family-run farms in the central and Northern states. The original towns now only accounted for 1 in 20 Americans, the largest of which – New York – had a population of just 20 000. However, this small urban society, largely composed of merchants, bankers and ship-owners, was dynamic and influential. In supporting Hamilton's theories of federalism, Washington and Adams acknowledged the importance of this aspect of society. According to Hamilton, the United States needed a strong federal government and an economy based on a system of capital production which encouraged investment. This would be facilitated by an industry built upon the manufacture of raw materials. At the same time, taxes on imports and the internal circulation of goods were introduced in order to finance the various governmental posts and to pay off the national debt incurred during the revolutionary war. It was within this context in 1791 that the Federal Bank of the United States was founded. In 1803, it would become the country's largest company with a foreign capital majority.

However, these decisions were not met with public approval; following the 1794 Whiskey Rebellion against a tax on distilled spirits, a new revolt erupted, lasting from 1798-1799. The situation worsened still when, during a period of tension between the US and France, Congress sought to increase defence spending. To do so, a new tax on land, housing and slaves was imposed. In Pennsylvania – a state composed largely of landed property-owners with few slaves – the tax weighed most heavily on housing, with value being calculated according to the number and size of doors and windows. The German settler community which cultivated the state's Southwestern territories mobilised against the surveyors and tax-collectors with auctioneer John Fries (1750-1818) at the helm. Fries was arrested along with other rebels in the spring of 1799 and sentenced to death by hanging, but was pardoned by President John Adams in 1800.

In the South, the legislation on imports also sparked controversy. The increase in the price of imported goods engendered similar reactionary policies in European countries, who in turn reduced their American imports.

THE QUASI-WAR WITH FRANCE

In 1793, the French Republic and Great Britain entered into war with one another. Consequently, Britain ordered the US to cease trade with France despite the Washington administration's public neutrality. American naval ships were quickly boarded and inspected by the Royal Navy and their crews threatened. The president therefore sought to diffuse the tension by signing a treating with Britain in 1794. While this pacified any ill feeling between the United States and the United Kingdom, it put Franco-American relations in a very precarious position. France considered the Anglo-American treaty as an act of hostility and retaliated by ordering American ships carrying British goods to be seized. The difficult task of managing this delicate situation was left to the new President John Adams, who at first approached it with diplomacy. However, Charles-Maurice de Talleyrand-Périgord (French politician, 1754-1838) refused to receive American emissaries, demanding a compensation payment if the slightest negotiation was to be made. The American government, feeling as though it was being held to ransom, refused to respond to French blackmail. John Adams went before Congress seeking approval for increased defence spending to prepare for the eventuality of armed conflict. He aimed to strengthen the navy and coastal defence, as well as establish a permanent army. Four bills, grouped under the heading The Alien and Sedition Acts were also proposed in 1798. The first of these – the Naturalisation Act – raised the waiting period for naturalisation from 5 to 14 years. The following two legislated for the deportation of non-American citizens who represented a threat to the nation or who came from a country with which America was at war. The fourth bill – the Sedition Act – legislated against any discourse critical of the American nation and its representatives. These laws provoked uproar among the Democratic-Republicans, who viewed them as encroaching on the basic freedoms guaranteed in the constitutional amendments.

Fighting between an American ship, the *USS Constellation*, and a French ship, *L'Insurgente*, on 9 February 1799.

The situation between France and America did not improve and incidences of hostility became more frequent in the Caribbean Sea, where the capture of both French and American ships seemed to herald an imminent conflict. However, when Napoleon Bonaparte assumed power in France, diplomatic relations improved and the Treaty of Morfontaine was signed in September 1800, officially ending the Quasi-War. Still, the conflict left an indelible mark which, when added to the economic problems of the time, led to Adams' defeat and Jefferson's victory in the 1801 presidential elections.

HIGHLIGHTS

A DIFFICULT FIRST ELECTION; AN UNCON-TESTED RE-ELECTION

Since his time as Secretary of State under George Washington, Jefferson had been the leader of the Democratic-Republican Party. Jefferson advocated a federal government with limited powers controlled by the people. This contrasted with the federalist perspective as outlined by Alexander Hamilton. Jefferson's approach endowed individual states with substantial power and thus emphasised individual liberties.

As John Adams' term drew to a close, discontentment with his federalist policy was rife. This was largely due to military spending on the Quasi-War, tax rises, and the Alien and Sedition Acts and everything which stemmed from them. John Adams, vying for a second term, struggled to rally popular support amidst Jefferson's virulent electoral campaign. Vicious personal attacks from competing newspapers polarised the debate: Jefferson was leading the country down a path of moral debauchery, whereas Adams was labelled as a tyrannical and foolish.

In the first round, Jefferson and his fellow candidate Aaron Burr (1756-1836) received 76 votes each, meaning 146 in total against the John Adams-Charles Pinckney (1757-1824) alliance's 130. Since the two Democratic-Republican candidates had tied, it was impossible to determine which of them should be president and which vice president.

It was not until the end of the 35th round with the help of Alexander Hamilton (who did not like Burr), that Jefferson was finally elected president.

GOOD TO KNOW

Aaron Burr, who became vice president, was a colourful character more renowned for his mischievous escapades than for his political activity. On 11 July 1804, he challenged Alexander Hamilton to a duel following insults levelled against him and killed him. With his political influence at rock-bottom, he fled and tried to found an independent state in 1805 in the Southern Spanish territories. Sent to trial for high treason in 1807, he left for Europe to find back-up and rebuild his fortune. He returned to New York in 1812, where he was to die in poverty several years later.

Jefferson's 1804 re-election ran much more smoothly. Selected once again as the Democratic-Republican candidate, he was up against Charles Pinckney, chosen only reluctantly by the Federalists. Public opinion towards Jefferson was largely favourable; he had indeed managed to stabilise the country's situation during his first term, and the attacks between the two candidates were much less aggressive than during the previous campaign. The Electoral College decisively endorsed Jefferson, with 162 votes to 14.

RESOLUTELY ANTI-FEDERALIST DOMESTIC POLICY

Staying true to his vision of a government which rarely intervened in the autonomous states' domestic affairs, Jefferson began by lowering federal spending. He reduced the size of the army and the navy, as well as the number of civil servants. In two years, he had cut the national debt by one quarter. He eliminated all domestic taxes, leaving taxes on imports as the only source of government revenue.

In 1802, he abolished the Alien and Sedition Acts to which he had been so strongly opposed and pardoned those who had been imprisoned under these laws. He equally changed naturalisation policy, setting the required period for citizenship at five years.

One year later, the legal world was shaken by the Marbury vs Madison case, which pitted Democrats and Republicans against one another and redefined the boundaries between executive and legislative power.

In 1801, William Marbury (1762-1835), a businessman with Federalist sympathies, was appointed as Justice of the Peace by President John Adams. The appointment of judges was one of the more discreet presidential powers. However, this particular appointment occurred in the final hours of his mandate and was interpreted as a politically motivated action to maintain a significant Federalist presence in the judiciary. When Jefferson came to power, he ordered his new Secretary of State James Madison not to deliver the commission to Marbury, his political adversary. When Marbury learned of this he brought the case before the Supreme Court, who ruled in his favour. The court ruled that not only did Marbury have the right to resort to legal action, the Secretary of State's actions (and by extension those of the president) were illegal; Marbury was within his rights to demand the delivery of his commission. However, while the Judiciary Act of 1789 gave him the right to receive it, the act itself was deemed unconstitutional by the court. In this case, the Supreme Court affirmed the absolute superiority of the constitution to all other laws and recognised from that point onwards the court's duty to scrutinise the constitutionality of all administrative acts and congressional laws.

On 25 September 1804, the 12th constitutional amendment was ratified, modifying the presidential election process. Where until that point one single vote covered the election of both president and vice president, with the candidate with the most votes taking the former title and the runner-up the latter, the new amendment created a different election for each post. This was due to the difficulties experienced during Jefferson's first election when he tied with Aaron Burr and the subsequent electoral rounds which this gave rise extreme tensions in the political community; the amendment sought to avoid any repeat of this unfortunate situation.

In terms of the economy, Thomas Jefferson distinguished himself from his predecessor by focusing on agricultural policy. He also championed territorial expansion in order to develop agriculture, which he considered the foundation of a solid and moral society, and criticised the way in which industry and money had corrupted Europe.

QUESTIONS ON SLAVERY AND THE TREATMENT OF NATIVE AMERICANS

Jefferson's paradoxical position on slavery came to light through his reflection on the creation of a vast agricultural empire. While he had continually denounced the way African-Americans were treated since the drafting of the Constitution, the cotton and tobacco trades needed a large workforce. As such, Jefferson himself kept nearly 600 slaves across his three plantations. Furthermore, while he considered enslaving and commodifying human beings to be revolting, he was not so convinced of the concept of racial equality. Such a viewpoint could be interpreted as active support for slavery, however he had in fact, prior to his presidency, taken it upon himself to ensure the Virginian Constitution codified the power of each slave-owner to individually emancipate his slaves. In fact, when his wife died, he fathered children with one of his slaves, Sally Hemings (c. 1773-1835).

However, while he supported the idea of individual emancipation and prohibited the import of slaves, he never truly addressed the question during his presidency. His ambiguous position is equally visible in his attitude towards integrating the African-American population as full citizens; he preferred the idea of creating a state in Africa for emancipated slaves.

Furthermore, Jefferson reaffirmed the legal requirement to deal and trade with Native Americans on even terms when buying their land. However, the United States' westward expansion and the purchase and exploration of Louisiana resulted in new and mounting tensions, particularly with regards to territorial negotiations. While the supposed intention of such efforts was to 'civilise' the indigenous population and integrate them into Jefferson's grand plan for American agriculture, in reality it came down to the Native Americans being dispossessed, stripped of their belongings and property and deported.

FOREIGN POLICY: THE PRESIDENT'S PREROGATIVE

Despite his wish to limit the federal government's powers and the Supreme Court's right to scrutinise certain decisions, Jefferson made foreign policy his personal prerogative and maintained the position of external neutrality established by the Federalists before him through his non-partisan foreign policy. He adopted no position on the conflicts which divided Europe to preserve his country's interests. When, however, these interests were threatened, he did not hesitate to intervene, as illustrated in the case of the Barbary Wars in the Mediterranean between 1801 and 1805. This intervention was aimed at addressing issues of piracy which were curtailing American and European maritime trade, despite the various accords which had been signed with the Ottoman Empire. In 1801, Jefferson refused a new financial demand issued by the Pasha of Tripoli. The Pasha reacted by destroying an American frigate – the *Philadelphia* – and the president decided to retaliate. Without seeking Congress's preliminary approval, the United States bombed Algiers and Tripoli. The operation was retrospectively approved by Congress, who decided to maintain a US Navy presence in the Mediterranean.

THE LOUISIANA PURCHASE

Jefferson's presidency was also marked by the Louisiana Purchase which allowed him to double the size of US territory. While Louisiana had belonged to France since 1682, the French were forced to surrender certain parts of the territory to Spain following the Treaty of Fontainebleau in 1762 and certain parts to Great Britain following the Treaty of Paris the following year. In 1800, Spain's position in its American colonies was weak. At the prospect of Bonaparte's rise to power it ceded the territory it had received several years previously back to France in the Treaty of San Ildefonso. The land in question was situated on the left bank of the Mississippi.

In fear of the French colonial empire knocking on his door and in hope of opening the river and gates of New Orleans to American trade and realising his agrarian dream, Jefferson secretly sent two emissaries to Paris. James Monroe (American statesman, 1758-1831) and Robert Livingston were charged with negotiating the purchase of New Orleans. To his great surprise, Bonaparte offered Jefferson all of Louisiana, fearing that conflict could break out there while he was busy fighting Great Britain in Europe; if such a situation were to occur, it was more or less certain that he would have been unable to defend the Louisianan territory against the British. As such, selling Louisiana was in fact a way of protecting this territory from British colonial ambitions. The operation was finally finished in April 1803: for 60 million francs and the cancellation of French debt, Jefferson acquired two million square kilometres of land. This transaction was, however, subject to criticism in both countries. In France, some were reluctant to give up on their colonial dreams, while in America, the Federalists – who advocated industry and the abolition of slavery as the pillars of the American economy – viewed the Louisiana Purchase as the triumph of the plantation economy and feared the effects it may have on relations with their number one trading partner - Great Britain. This in addition to the fact that Jefferson had not consulted Congress before beginning the negotiations showed once again Jefferson's presidential prerogative as he took on powers not outlined in the constitution.

Hoisting American Colors Over Louisiana, painting by Thure de Thulstrup, c. 1904.

THE LEWIS AND CLARK EXPEDITION AND THE CONQUEST OF THE WEST

Louisiana having been acquired, Jefferson, a man fascinated by discovery and science, was motivated to expand the young nation of the United States. In 1804 he launched a major expedition to discover the "New World", with Meriwether Lewis and William Clark, infantry lieutenant and Lewis's friend, leading the Corps of Discovery. The two men prepared themselves for their mission by consulting texts written by woodsmen and trappers, and set off in spring 1804 from Camp Dubois at the mouth of the Mississippi river near St. Louis. They took around 30 men with them, as well as gifts and armaments to prepare for any encounters with Native Americans.

GOOD TO KNOW

The expedition team counted among its number a woodsman named Toussaint Charbonneau (1767-1843), a man of Canadian and Sioux Native American origin and his partner Sacagawea. She herself was from the Shoshones nation but had been taken by Minnetaree people when she was just ten. She proved to be a vital asset and a peacekeeper among this troop of men; she had great knowledge of the land and was able to interpret and mediate when they came into contact with Native American communities. During the journey, she found her tribe and her brother, but decided to continue the mission with the other explorers. Though

The explorers followed the river paths and waters in canoes and spent two years crossing the continent right up to the Pacific coast, travelling through modern-day Missouri, Illinois and Kansas. They then crossed over the Rocky Mountains for the first time and came across many indigenous communities. It was a true quest; they battled and overcame the cold, sickness, and perilous adventures like the treacherous peaks of the Lolo Trail on the massive Bitterroot Ridge (Idaho) or river rapids and waterfalls. In an episode known as the Great Portage, the adventurers were even forced to scale the rock-face carrying their canoes and equipment to cross the Great Falls of the Missouri River. They reached the edge of the Pacific in December 1805 at the mouth of the Columbia River (Oregon), and spent the winter there before beginning their homeward journey. When spring came, Lewis and Clark separated so one could explore the Marias River at the Canadian border and the other the Yellowstone River in Montana. They met once again at the mouth of the Yellowstone River a few months later and were back in St. Louis by September 1806.

During the two-and-a-half-year period, the explorers surveyed the wildlife they came across and mapped the new territory. The newly-discovered lands were then acquired through negotiations or by force from the Native Americans and divided into territories defined by natural borders. They were then divided into lots by the government and sold to the settlers. Once a territory's population had reached the figure cited in the Northwestern Ordinance (60 000) and republican institutions had been introduced, they could claim the title of state. This expedition and process not only quenched Jefferson's thirst for knowledge and understanding, but allowed him to realise his grand political designs of establishing the world's largest republic.

IMPACT

As the first Democratic-Republican president, Jefferson made his mark in many ways. First and foremost, he tried to turn the United States into his vision of a republic; a federal government with limited powers, made for and by a moral and virtuous society of landowners with an agricultural economy.

While he reduced the central concentration of power, he nonetheless showed the powers of the president to be of major importance in his occasional skirting of the constitution. Furthermore, his commitment to the republican ideal led him to act contrary to his own political convictions on several occasions as he sought to provide for the common good of the nation. When Jefferson was forced to toe the line in the Marbury vs. Madison case, he actually helped establish one of the fundamental elements of the modern US judiciary – the Supreme Court's power of judicial review.

Jefferson was a man and a president of paradoxes, as demonstrated by his attitude towards slavery. While he denounced the exploitation of African-Americans, his agrarian vision of the nation was strongly dependent on slave labour. He also supported the idea of creating an African state in which emancipated slaves could live freely, an idea which equally raises questions surrounding racial integration in American society. Such a project was eventually put into action by the American Colonization Society led by Congressman Henry Clay (American politician, 1777-1852), with the creation of the city of Monrovia and, in 1847, the Republic of Liberia. However, the question was left unanswered on American soil by both Jefferson and his successors, who instead aggravated the problem through a project of territorial expansion which at once raised issues regarding enslaved workforces involved in the project and sparked significant tensions with Native American populations. African and Native Americans made up the majority of the US population, though received none of the benefits of citizenship – this situation continually worsened and 50 years later it led to the American Civil War and the American Indian Wars.

Jefferson sought to remain externally neutral, particularly with regards to Franco-British conflict in Europe. However, he was unable to achieve such neutrality; his decisions led to a financial crisis and war. While he was successful in strictly limiting federal government expenses during his first term and thus reducing the national debt, he nonetheless led the American economy into a major crisis through the Embargo Act which had a severe impact on import-export commerce. Britain reacted to the restrictions placed upon their ships in this act by blocking America's trade with other European nations and supporting the Native American side during conflicts in the newly-acquired Western territories of the US. The significant Anglo-American tensions which had accumulated by the end of the Jefferson administration were one of the factors leading to the War of 1812 between the two nations.

Jefferson's vision of territorial expansion also gave way to disillusionment. He saw the acquisition of Louisiana and

Lewis and Clark's exploration of this vast territory as the realisation of his republican dream of an egalitarian society based on small landowners and agriculture. In fact, it indirectly contributed to a major land speculation movement which deprived the poorest of land to cultivate, pushing them further westward still. The government continued to exercise power over territories increasingly far from the federal epicentre, giving rise to problems with the Native American nations which would last for decades; Jefferson made a significant effort to pacify this relationship.

Jefferson is without a doubt a complex figure to assess. He found himself caught between the ideals and philosophy of the Enlightenment and the practical reality of power which marked out his administration as one in a true state of flux.

SUMMARY

1743
13th Apr.: Birth of Thomas Jefferson

1755-1783
War of Independence

1789-1795
Serves as Secretary of State in
Washington administration

1801
4th Mar.: **Inaugurated as President**

1803
Apr.: Louisiana Purchase

1804
Lewis and Clark Expedition

1805
4th Mar.: Inaugurated for second
presidential term

1809
4th Mar.: **James Madison inaugurated
as President**

1819
University of Virginia officially opens

1826
4th July: Death of Jefferson

- Thomas Jefferson was born in 1743, and began his career at the Virginia bar in 1767.
- Jefferson was more renowned for his writing talents than his skills as an orator: he was the principal author of the Declaration of Independence, adopted by the Continental Congress on 4 July 1776.
- In January 1789, Jefferson was appointed Secretary of State by the newly elected President George Washington.
- Jefferson became increasingly involved in politics and became the leader of the Democratic-Republican Party. He advocated a federal government with limited powers checked by the electorate and strong autonomous states. As such, he placed a strong emphasis on individual liberty.
- Seven years later, Jefferson stood in the presidential elections but was defeated by John Adams, who did not share his political views. He was nonetheless appointed vice president.
- Jefferson became the third President of the United States in February 1801 and was re-elected four years later.
- During his presidency, he managed to reduce the national debt by curbing military spending, and abolished the taxes responsible for riots under his predecessors.
- His attitude towards the crucial question of slavery was paradoxical. While he actively participated in discouraging and limiting the maltreatment and exploitation of African-Americans and entrenched the right to emancipate individual slaves in the state of Virginia, his dreams of an agricultural empire relied strongly on slave labour.
- When he attempted to purchase New Orleans from France in 1803, Napoleon Bonaparte offered to sell him

the whole state of Louisiana for an attractive price. Through this acquisition, Jefferson doubled the surface area of American territory.

- Jefferson was passionate about discovery, and launched an exploration mission one year after the Louisiana Purchase. He sent his personal adviser Meriwether Lewis and William Clark to lead the Corps of Discovery into the New World for over two years, to survey the wildlife and create new maps. The territories they explored were bought by the Americans, divided into territories and sold by lots to the settlers.
- When his second term came to an end, Jefferson decided to retire from politics and return home to dedicate himself to founding the University of Virginia.

We want to hear from you!
Leave a comment on your online library
and share your favourite books on social media!

FIND OUT MORE

BIBLIOGRAPHY

- Brenda, P. and Lentz, T. (2006) Napoléon. *L'esclavage et les colonies*. Paris: Fayard.
- Bruce, D. K. (1954) *Les présidents des USA de George Washington à Abraham Lincoln*. Paris: Gallimard.
- Bureau international de l'économie américaine. (2012). *Esquisse de l'économie américaine*. Paris: Belin.
- Desbiens, A. (2012) *Histoire des États-Unis. Des origines à nos jours*. Paris: Éditions du Nouveau Monde.
- Fohlen, C. (1992) *Thomas Jefferson*. Nancy: Presses universitaires de Nancy.
- Freidel, F. and Sidey, H. (2006) Thomas Jefferson. *The Presidents of the United States of America*. Washington: The White House Historical Association.
- Kaspi, A. (1972) *La naissance des États-Unis. Révolution ou guerre d'indépendance?* Paris: Presses universitaires de France.
- Lagayette, P. (2002) *Thomas Jefferson et l'Ouest: L'expédition de Lewis et Clark*. Paris: Ellipses.
- Meyer, J. (2009) *L'Europe et la conquête du monde, XVIe-XVIIe siècles*. Paris: Armand Colin.
- Miller Center of Public Affairs, University of Virginia. (2016) *Thomas Jefferson*. [Online]. [Accessed 13 March 2017]. Available from: <https://millercenter.org/president/jefferson>
- Portes, J. (2010) *Histoire des États-Unis. De 1776 à nos jours*. Paris: Armand Colin.

ADDITIONAL SOURCES

- Meacham, J. (2013) *Thomas Jefferson: The Art of Power*. New York: Random House Publishing Group.
- Seavoy, R. (2006) *An Economic History of the United States from 1607 to the Present*. New York: Routledge.

ICONOGRAPHIC SOURCES

- Portrait of Thomas Jefferson by Mather Brown. Royalty-free reproduction picture.
- Photograph of Monticello as it currently stands. © Martin Falbisoner.
- *Writing the Declaration of Independence, 1776*, painting by Jean Leon Gerome Ferris, depicting (from left to right) Benjamin Franklin, John Adams and Thomas Jefferson. Royalty-free reproduction picture.
- Fighting between an American ship, the *USS Constellation*, and a French ship, *L'Insurgente*, on 9 February 1799. Royalty-free reproduction picture.
- *Hoisting American Colors Over Louisiana*, painting by Thure de Thulstrup, c. 1904. Royalty-free reproduction picture.

FILMS AND DOCUMENTARIES

- *Jefferson in Paris*. (1995) [Film]. James Ivory. Dir. France, USA: Touchstone Pictures.
- *Thomas Jefferson*. (1997) [Mini-series]. Ken Burns. Dir. USA: American Lives Film Project.
- *Lewis & Clark: Great Journey West*. (2002)

[Documentary]. USA: National Geographic.

MUSEUM

- Thomas Jefferson's house (Virginia, USA).

IMPROVE YOUR GENERAL KNOWLEDGE

IN A BLINK OF AN EYE !

www.50minutes.com